PORTSMOUTH

↠ *Yesterday and Today* ↞

ANTHONY TRIGGS

HALSGROVE

First published in Great Britain in 1997
Reprinted in 1999 and 2001

British Library Cataloguing in Publication Data

A CIP record for this book is available from the British Library

ISBN 1 874448 31 0

HALSGROVE
Halsgrove House
Lower Moor Way
Tiverton
Devon EX16 6SS
Tel: 01884 243242
Fax: 01884 243325
www.halsgrove.com

Printed in Great Britain by Hackman Print, Rhondda

Contents

Acknowledgements

great many people can become involved in compiling a book of this nature, and I would like to thank those who have taken both the time and trouble to help, starting with my publisher, Steven Pugsley, for giving me the opportunity to compile this new collection of images.

Researching pictures is the biggest part of most local history writers' work, so my thanks go to those who have come to my aid. Firstly I must thank Geoffrey Elliott, editor of the *News*, Portsmouth, for allowing me to use pictures from the newspaper's collection, which appear on pages 28, 32, 72, 82, 84 and 94. Also Sarah Quail and her most helpful staff at Portsmouth City Museum and Record Office, for pictures which appear on pages 20, 26, 38, 40, 60, 76, 78 and 86.

Other friends who have helped include June Long, Carol Farr, Martin Petch, Tom Dethridge (who provided the picture on page 33), Mike Smith, Frank Naylor, Tony Gregory, Eric Watts, and the unnamed young lady in the Commercial Road branch of H. Samuel, who allowed me to take pictures from the shop's upstairs storeroom. Finally there is a debt of gratitude which is my greatest pleasure to acknowledge – that to my wife Sue whose help and encouragement is ever present.

Introduction

ack in 1984 I had the good fortune to have been invited to compile a little book which was designed to show how the great city of Portsmouth had changed over the years.

It was a labour of love for it gave me the unrivalled opportunity to combine effectively two of my interests – local history and photography.

The book was called *Portsmouth Past and Present*, and it presented 50 vintage photographs of the city and paired each one with a modern counterpart, taken from as near to the original viewpoint that I could get.

Since then the book has been reprinted twice, and has sold in excess of 12,000 copies, many going to far-flung corners of the world.

And a follow-up volume, *Portsmouth Then and Now*, brought a second selection into focus.

Now the opportunity has presented itself for a new collection, and as in the past I have tried to research the old pictures so as to provide those that are predominantly fresh to my readers.

It is very easy to gather together a number of old post-cards, but in many cases they will have been seen before in other publications.

After all the golden age of postcards only started in 1894 – when the post office licensed the use of picture cards – and ended in about 1918. Although many cards were produced in subsequent years, the earlier period was the most prolific.

So to avoid duplication with other authors' books I have tried to be a little different.

The earliest picture in this current collection is from about 1870, and the baby of the bunch dates from 1972, which, after all, is still a quarter of a century ago!

I have also included a selection taken in the immediate post-war period, showing graphically the ravages caused by the German bombs.

The modern pictures show how the city has changed – how the post-war development programme has dramatically altered the Portsmouth that many of us knew in the past.

Whether these mental images are from long ago, or from just around the corner of our memories, they serve to show how the years have treated our proud city.

Portsmouth author and illustrator Richard Esmond – who years ago encouraged me in my interest in Portsmouth past – summed up his thoughts in the foreword to his 1961 book *Portsmouth Not So Old*.

He wrote: 'These notes are a small attempt to recapture some echoes of those earlier days for people who still remember them, and perhaps for some who are not old enough to remember, but are still interested in the story of their own city. I know there are many of both sorts, and all are conscious. like St Paul, that they are "citizens of no mean city".'

These sentiments still apply thirty-six years on!

Anthony Triggs, Portchester, 1997

Passengers disembark from a Gosport to Portsmouth ferry at the pontoon near Portsmouth Harbour railway station. The number of parasols in evidence indicate that it was a hot and sunny day. The vessel unloading is one of the early boats, probably owned by the Portsmouth Watermen's Steam Launch Company, one of the original groups that eventually merged to form one larger company. The rail viaduct curves out towards the south railway jetty where a businesslike warship is lying alongside. Today the viaduct is no more, but HMS *Warrior* recreates an aura of Victorian elegance.

Trams and taxis wait for passengers at The Hard, Portsmouth. In 1934 a swimming pool for children was opened near the main gate to the dockyard. To the left, almost hidden by a building, is one of the futuristic Karrier single-deck buses which proved to be so troublesome, and were consequently taken out of service after only a few years in 1936. The area today is the focus for visitors to the dockyard heritage area, and for travellers to the Isle of Wight.

Queen Street – named after Queen Anne – was always the main artery from the dockyard to the town, and became known for its brothels and beer houses. In the '20s Portsmouth began a huge slum clearance operation, and many of the tiny alleys and passages disappeared. More were to go in the war years. Now the area has given way to tourism, with HMS *Victory*, HMS *Warrior*, and the *Mary Rose* drawing the visitors.

This between-the-wars picture shows the view from Hawke Street to Queen Street. Hawke Street was named after naval hero Admiral Sir Edward Hawke, and was to be widened as part of the Portsea clearance programme, sparked by the murder of prostitute Brighton Mary in a hovel in Blossom Alley. The ensuing outcry led to the building of Portsmouth's first purpose-built council dwellings, some of the earliest of which can be seen at the left of the picture. Now Hawke Street faces out to a very different Queen Street, used by thousands of visitors to the dockyard.

Ratings are seen outside the imposing gateway to the Portsmouth Naval barracks – HMS *Nelson*. The barracks were opened in September 1889 and were considered at the time to be the most modern and durable quarters in the country. They were built on the site of the old corporation stoneyard and the Anglesea Barracks. Views of the inside were restricted by the tin sheeting which was erected following a near-riot sparked by a series of misunderstandings. The unsightly addition remained until 1956. The barracks now have a modern open outlook.

In the days before the war, and certainly in the austere days just after the war, the morning market at Unicorn Road was a popular place to buy and sell clothes. Families with little income could, at least, clothe their children cheaply, even though most of the garments were third hand. The much-reduced market continued until Unicorn Road was redeveloped with the city's new road system.

Victoria Park was created on the old Portsea glacis in 1878. It became known as the people's park, and provided a green and pleasant haven from the growing traffic for holidaymakers, residents, and shoppers. It was officially opened by the mayor, William King, and within its 15 acres are trees, shrubs and a hothouse. It is also home for a number of memorials recalling naval battles.

In 1895 the *Evening News* moved from its old headquarters in Arundel Street to new purpose-built offices in Stanhope Road, remaining there until 1969 when another great change took place with the move to the News Centre at Hilsea. The picture shows the view directly after the war, with the newspaper office unscathed. However the brick rubble in the right of the picture indicates the damage done to the Connaught Drill Hall. Today the huge black reflective Zurich Insurance building stands on the newspaper office site.

This is the once-familiar gateway to the Royal Portsmouth Hospital, which was opened in 1849, and cost £2310 to build. As health care in the city expanded the hospital followed suit and new wards and wings were added. The gateway, known by so many patients over the years, was built in 1921 and was opened by Princess Victoria. The hospital finally closed in 1979 and now a filling station and a branch of Sainsbury's cover the site. The company has ensured that a tangible reminder of the hospital remains with a foundation plaque from the original building preserved in the supermarket foyer.

A royal occasion was always a good excuse for the gateway to the Gunwharf to be decorated, and here it is dressed for the diamond jubilee of Queen Victoria in 1897. The Gunwharf was originally an army base, used for the storage of ordnance and shot. It was taken over by the navy in 1923 and housed the torpedo school HMS *Vernon*, which previously had been based aboard a number of hulks moored up-harbour. Now the 30-acre area is to get new life when the £120m refurbishment plan for the millennium regeneration of Portsmouth Harbour takes place.

The bell loft in the spire of the Guildhall proved a vantage point for an enterprising cameraman in 1906. Dominating the picture is the imposing Central Hotel which was gutted during the blitz in 1941, and was demolished for safety reasons the following year. Willis Road can be seen between the Connaught Drill Hall and the rear of the Speedwell Hotel. At the bottom right is the old general post office, built in 1883 and pulled down in 1978 during the city centre redevelopment programme. Far in the background, to the left, is the Rudmore gas holder. Today's picture, taken from the same viewpoint, shows a different panorama, although the Connaught Drill Hall – rebuilt after the war – is still in the same position.

It's business as usual in a rather desolated post-war Commercial Road. The Guildhall with its flat-top look dominates the skyline. To the left is Arundel Street, with areas of waste ground where once stood shops. The Landport Drapery Bazaar, now Allders, was destroyed during the war, but rose again from the ashes during the great rebuilding of the city. This part of Commercial Road is now a pedestrian precinct.

The imposing Speedwell Hotel stood on the corner of Commercial Road and Stanhope Road. It was one of the city's grandest establishments, and being situated so near to the railway station, it was extremely popular with visitors. Note the line of barrows parked in Stanhope Road, upon which the porters would convey guests' luggage to the station. The area was redeveloped and city centre shops now occupy the site.

This is Russell Street between the wars, looking towards the Guildhall Square. To the left is Swan Street, which ran into Commercial Road opposite the White Swan public house. Further up Russell Street can just be discerned Salem Street. Russell Street was swallowed up in the city centre redevelopment and the building of the civic offices. Alec Rose Lane now stands on part of the line of Swan Street, although now it terminates in the renamed Guildhall Walk.

Post-war high-rise housing development is already apparent in this 1968 photograph of the Guildhall Square. Russell Street can be seen at the top left of the picture, while on the right the now blocked-off Park Road is still a straight route to the Gunwharf and the Hard. Five years earlier Lord Esher had been appointed by the city council as consulting architect for the regeneration of the Guildhall area. His brief was to provide central offices for the city council, and to develop a central city core worthy of the size and importance of Portsmouth. The modern Guildhall Square links old and new – with the smoked glass of the civic offices reflecting the magnificence of the Guildhall itself.

Greetham Street, which led to the Guildhall Square by way of the imposing Sussex Hotel, is pictured here after the war. Before 1939 the road had been a useful adjunct to the railway goods yard which was originally sited next to the town station. At the Guildhall Square end a number of meat processing plants were situated – again the proximity of the railway line made Greetham Street a favourite location. Now much of the street is lost beneath the civic offices, and the remaining part has been redeveloped for housing. The modern view is taken from the Jacob's Ladder railway footbridge.

This unprepossessing view taken in the early '70s shows the part of the original Commercial Road blocked off because of the construction of Market Way. Now this little piece of the former main artery through Portsmouth is a conservation area. All Saints church can now hardly be seen because of the trees, and the Mile End Cellars still stands, although under the new name of the Oliver Twist. The name reflects the fact that the area contains the house which is the birthplace of Charles Dickens – now a museum.

Tramcar No 10 negotiates the busy interchange at Bradford Junction, Southsea, in September 1936. The tram – which is using the new trolleybus wires for power – is running on the service 6 route from the Dockyard to South Parade Pier, via Milton and Eastney. On the right is the Plaza cinema, which later became the Gaumont, and was latterly a bingo hall. The original cinema was opened in 1928 and was considered to be the most luxurious picture palace in the city. It showed Portsmouth's first talking picture, and was the first cinema to open on Sundays. The picture house became a bingo hall in 1965, but by 1997 dwindling attendances forced it to close. At the time of writing the listed building is awaiting a buyer.

The legacy of the blitz is still evident in this 1955 picture of Cambridge Junction. High Street, Old Portsmouth, is straight ahead with the Portsmouth Grammar School on the left. The school is housed in the former Cambridge Barracks which it took over in the '20s. On the far left of the picture is Alexandra Road. The city museum is now housed in another part of the garrison complex – Clarence Barracks – and the road has subsequently been renamed Museum Road.

Sally Port and the hot walls was, and still is, a popular place to swim and sunbathe, with the historic Round Tower in the background. On the opposite side of the harbour mouth the tallest building is Holy Trinity church, nowadays completely hidden by the high-rise flats. The training ship *Foudroyant* in moored at the harbour mouth. Once ships of the line could be seen coming and going about their business – now it is cross-channel ferries that dominate the sea view.

This, the oldest view in the book, shows Pembroke Road looking towards High Street in 1870, just ten years after the demolition of the King William Gate. The structure was built in 1833 to give a gateway from the fortified town to the rapidly expanding area of Southsea. Higher up Pembroke Road is the Royal Naval Yacht Club, seen here before its observation tower was built. Now only the gatehouse of the gate remains, on the left of the modern picture, to record the structure's passing.

High Street has always been the main road from Old Portsmouth to the newer modern city. It is pictured here at the turn of the century before redevelopment and the war took its toll. Many of the buildings on the left of the picture were cleared to form Cathedral Green when Portsmouth was elevated to a city, and St Thomas's Church became the cathedral. Further along the street is the George Hotel where Nelson spent his last hours before embarking for Trafalgar. His room was retained as a museum piece, but all was lost when German bombs destroyed the hotel.

Intending passengers wait while those arriving disembark from a tram at Pier Road, Southsea, near Clarence Pier. This point had been the terminus of the original horse tramway of 1865, which transferred rail passengers from the town station to the Isle of Wight ferries waiting at the pier. The lamp standard was said to have been made from one of the original gas standards which had been removed from its site in St George's Square. The Pier Road junction is still a busy arrival point for island-bound travellers, but now the hovercraft does the journey in a fraction of the ferry crossing time.

The Esplanade Hotel was converted in 1877 from the former King's Rooms, originally built as assembly rooms and baths. The hotel was constructed entirely of timber because it would have been in the line of fire from the guns of the Portsmouth garrison, and in time of attack could have been easily demolished to provide the gunners with an uninterrupted view of the target. Today a futuristic amusement venue stands on the site amid the cluster of seaside shops.

43

Clarence Pier presents an imposing structure in this view from about 1890. The pier was opened in 1861 to cater for the Isle of Wight steamer trade, relying on the horse-drawn tram from Portsmouth. The glass-sided pavilion was opened in 1882. When the harbour station link was opened a great deal of the island traffic was lost. The pier was almost totally destroyed in the war but has reopened to provide modern entertainment in conjunction with the fairground.

The beach at Clarence Esplanade in Edwardian times presents a busy scene, with parasols and hats in proliferation. The promenade was officially opened in 1848 and was named after the former governor of Portsmouth garrison, Lord Frederick Fitzclarence, who was instrumental in having it constructed. As a child he had overheard the words of his father, the Duke of Clarence, who remarked that 'an admirable promenade can be made of Southsea beach.' Today the promenade is a great attraction for holidaymakers and residents alike.

The bandstand on Southsea Common was built in 1924 as part of the redevelopment plan for the huge area of land which was purchased from the War Department in 1922. The council resolved to spend £60,000 on converting what was described as a miniature Sahara into gardens and playgrounds. The bandstand was very popular in the '20s and '30s, with the wide apron around it being used for dancing. In the immediate post-war years it took on a new guise as a roller-skating rink, and is now given over to skateboard users.

This commercial postcard view shows what was then called the New South Parade Pier. This dates the card at somewhat after 1908, the year in which the pier was opened following the destruction of the earlier 'fire-proof' 1879 structure. The new pier survived unscathed until 1974 when it was all but destroyed when fire broke out during the filming of Ken Russell's rock opera *Tommy*. However, the pier rose again from the ashes and is still a popular venue for holidaymakers.

The Ladies' Mile on Southsea Common is still a popular place for strolling, walking the dog, or just taking the air. Although nowhere near a mile in length, the asphalt walk got its name because of the young ladies who provided a beauty and fashion display after church on a Sunday morning. The National Union of Teachers' conference souvenir for Easter 1937 said the Sunday-morning visitor 'will soon agree the "a miss" is as good as "a mile".' Sadly many of the fine trees were lost to Dutch elm disease, and many more fell in the great storm of 1987, which left this part of Southsea looking like the aftermath of war. Now new trees are taking their place.

The rock gardens at Southsea were created in the '20s as part of the redevelopment of the common. The council reported that the gardens 'would, in size, rival any that have been artificially constructed in Great Britain.' In the background of the picture is the Rock Gardens Pavilion, which was eventually taken down in favour of the Pyramids Centre – a water–based family attraction, which can be seen in the modern picture.

Fifties youngsters take to the water in the children's paddling pool which was situated to the west of Southsea Castle. The pool was built in 1928 when Southsea Common was improved to form a popular open space. Times change, however, and the pool was lost in the 1980s when the Sea Life Centre complex was built.

The old Dock Mill stands tall – a monument to a brave attempt at an early co-operative movement. The windmill was built in 1816 by a group of shipwrights who formed the Dockyard Mill Society and Bread Company. However, by 1834 the business was in difficulties and the mill was shut down, standing derelict until 1869, when it was bought by enterprising miller Maurice Welch. The mill lasted until 1923 when it was demolished, and now only the cottages remain. They too were threatened with demolition, but were restored.

The fashionable department store of Handleys was destroyed in the war, but it rose again on its original site. The ornate building of the National and Provincial Bank of England can be seen at the right of the picture. Immediately after the war the Handleys' site was cleared and the council laid it out as temporary flower gardens until such time as the rebuilding work could start. Today the store is part of the huge Debenhams empire.

Osborne Road, still a popular shopping street, was originally named Osborne View, probably because of its panoramic outlook across the Solent to the Isle of Wight. Traffic was a lot easier for pedestrians to negotiate, and although there is no trolleybus in sight, the overhead wires bear witness to those silent public transport vehicles, introduced into Portsmouth in 1934. They were eventually phased out in 1963.

This superb view is from the 1880s, and shows the original Palmerston Road shops, with a neatly-labelled Stanley Street running off to the right. In the background is the spire of Thomas Ellis Owen's magnificent St Jude's church, the only building left standing after the blitz. The shopping centre was rebuilt and is now a popular pedestrian precinct.

Elm Grove once was a tree-lined thoroughfare, originally called Wish Lane. In Victorian times Elm Grove became a high-class residential area with imposing houses hidden behind the lines of beautiful elms after which it was named. Despite an outcry these homes were demolished in favour of shops, and the last elm was cut down in 1931, provoking another outcry at what was described as the 'desecration' of the city. The shops still remain in this busy area which is a popular feeder road into Southsea.

Castle Road once ran from Southsea to the popular shopping centre at Kings Road, and was supposedly named from the Castle public house which stood on the corner. The Kings Road shopping centre was totally destroyed in the war, but in its heyday it boasted a variety of shops including the department store of John Dyer, at the time considered to be the biggest in Southsea.

Marmion Road, one of the lesser shopping streets of Southsea, was named after the house of an early landowner, Jonathan Webb. Webb owned the entire northern frontage of the road in addition to Webb's Marshes, an area of land around the present Victoria Road which was mostly under water. In the background of both pictures is St Jude's, now covered in scaffolding and screening and undergoing a £1m refurbishment programme following a public appeal.

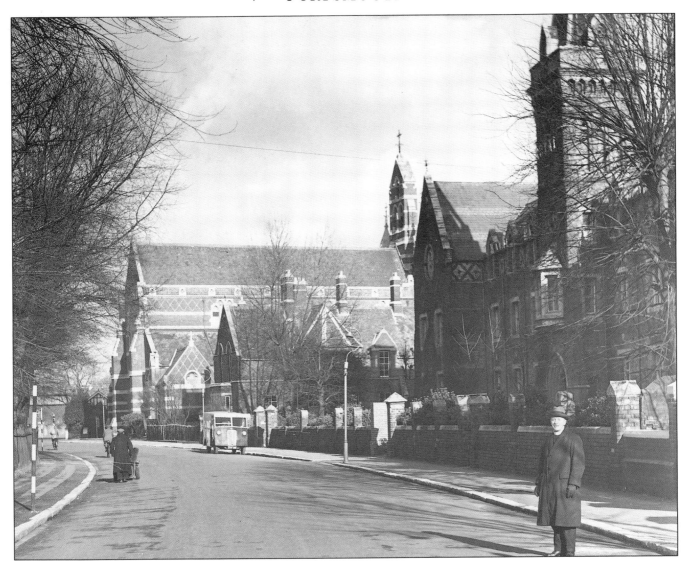

The imposing church of St Michael and All Angels dominates this view of St Michael's Road. The church was designed by William Butterfield and cost £20,000. Building commenced in 1872, but ten years later at the time of consecration, only half of the building had been completed. It took a further ten years to finish. Although situated near the dockyard, St Michael's survived the blitz, but eventually became a victim of roads redevelopment, and was demolished in 1960. The site is now occupied by a University of Portsmouth building.

Landport Terrace is part of a line of similar buildings – Hampshire Terrace, Kings Terrace and Jubilee Terrace – which led from the city to the affluent residential area of Southsea. Traditionally the home of solicitors, its role has changed very little. Today the traffic is different, and the buildings on the Kings Road corner are new, but this part of town varies only minimally.

Before the war Southsea boasted a number of fine residential roads containing villa type residences. Ashburton Road was one. Here the road is in a sorry state following the excesses of the German bombing. However, as the modern-day view shows, many of the old buildings were saved with only a small amount of modern construction. This area, off Palmerston Road, is now part of the city's 'bedsit land.'

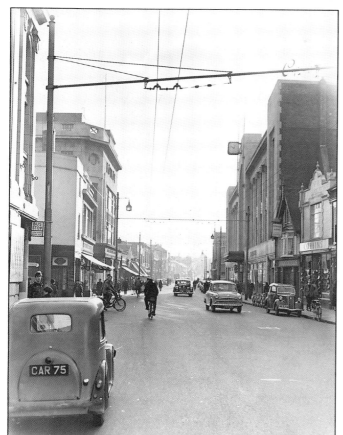

Car 75 where are you? This evocative picture shows Fratton Road in those post-war days when retail trading in the area was mainly in the hands of the Portsea Island Co-operative Society. On the right is the society's flagship store, Co-operative House, with its distinctive clock. The first store on the site was destroyed by fire in 1934, and was rebuilt only to be in ruins again as a result of the terrible night of bombing on 10 January, 1941. It was rebuilt yet again, but since then the society has changed with the times and a new shopping mall, the Bridge Centre, stands on the site of the once magnificent Co-operative House.

It is 1972 and the redevelopment of the city centre is well under way. This is the eastern end of Arundel Street before the construction of the ring road. The tiny shops are still in business, although their time was running out as they were soon to be demolished. On the right are the narrow turnings into what was Claxton Street and Mary Street. The site is now occupied by a school.

A quiet day in Milton, looking northwards up Milton Road. The road sign to Milton Park Road can be seen on the right, while in the distance is the church-like library building. A 1930 Leyland Titan bus is making its leisurely way towards the camera. Now the road is a busy thoroughfare lined with shops and houses, although Milton Park, on the left, is still a green haven.

It's roadworks time outside Kingston Prison in 1931 as the finishing touches are made to the road after the building of the shelter and public toilets. The forbidding prison itself was built in 1879 at a cost of £35,000. The castellated construction is of Plymouth stone with Doulton stone dressings. By 1931 the prison was closed because of government changes, but within a few years its use was again recognised and it was reopened. It fulfills a similar role today.

Mud, mud, glorious mud would have been an appropriate tune for Randolph Road, North End, in 1930. Some of the roads in the new development had not yet been properly finished, and a particularly long spell of wet weather had left these homes surrounded by a sea of mire. Residents had been complaining and eventually the work was completed. It is interesting to note on the modern picture how little the line of the houses has changed in the intervening sixty-seven years.

To a certain extent this view of North End is very much as we know it now. At the centre of London Road and Gladys Avenue is the house which was to be replaced by the bus company offices. On the corner of Stubbington Avenue once stood North End House, the residence of Sir John Baker, former MP for Portsmouth, who died in 1909. The gabled building to the right is White's furniture repository.

This line of modern houses in Copnor Road was photographed in 1930, a mere two or three years after completion. Although it is interesting to look back on such a picture, it is puzzling to understand why it was chosen as a commercial postcard. Copnor Road is now a busy thoroughfare and carries traffic in far greater numbers than could ever have been imagined in the '30s.

The original Coach and Horses public house is pictured here before demolition in 1931. The painting on the wall can be seen clearly. It depicts a stagecoach being held up with a poetic caption likening the highwayman to Herbert Asquith, the chancellor of the exchequer. A new hostelry was built and the painting was reproduced in painted tiles, which can be seen today. The inn has recently undergone a complete refurbishment.

This picture from the peaceful days of the 1930s shows Port Creek in a different light. Highbury estate is still undergoing construction, and much of the building materials would have been brought in by water. Today Tudor Crescent, to the left of the picture, is still there, although hidden by the A27 flyover, which carries thousands of vehicles every day into the city or on to the M27.

The complex series of overhead wires at Portsbridge, Hilsea, was needed to separate the traffic near the Southdown garage. From this point trolley buses went to Northern Parade, Copnor Road, and London Road. Today the garage is a depot for the Co-operative Dairies, with modern footbridges crossing the busy multi-lane road.

Cosham became part of Portsmouth in 1920 along with Paulsgrove, and a memorial milestone was unveiled by the mayor, Councillor John Timpson. This commercial postcard dates from about 1905. The camera is facing northwards, and Waite Street is on the left of the picture. A number of people have obviously stopped in order to be recorded for posterity, although the cows, further up the street, seem totally disinterested. Cosham today is a busy suburb.

At first glance the scene in Northern Road, Cosham, appears to have changed very little since 1952 when the earlier photograph was taken. Two significant features are the absence of the flats in the background, and the arrival of the footbridge from the police station to the former post office. The post office has now moved to Cosham High Street.

The year is 1971 and work on the ill-fated Portsdown Park is continuing with the construction of the first of its three giant tower blocks. The first tenants moved in in 1975, but the project was dogged with problems. Residents complained of water penetration, damp and vandalism and eventually the city council cut its losses and in 1987 decided the estate should go. Now a grouping of exclusive homes stands on the site.

The annual fair has come to the hillslopes, and here pleasure seekers are seen on their way. The war is at its height, as can be judged from the proliferation of gas mask holders. The helpful constable on traffic duty is also prepared, as the steel helmet shows. The Horndean Light Railway bridge can be seen spanning the Southwick Hill Road. Now, on today's busy road, the fair and the tramway are but memories, recalling earlier simple pleasures and pastimes.

Interested spectators gather in 1930 outside the George Inn to watch what looks suspiciously like an early car rally. A policeman directs the traffic, and an ice cream seller, to the right of the picture, is obviously on to a winner. Nowadays a more complicated road layout eases the traffic at the inn, and much of the rough grassland has been landscaped.

In the early post-war days the council continued its policy of spreading the boundaries of the city, and the Paulsgrove 'colony' was a prime example. Here in 1949 at the Broadway, the shopkeepers, including the Portsea Island Co-operative Society, are trading from Nissen huts with just brick frontages. As the estate grew these temporary units disappeared and new purpose-built shops were constructed.

This view from Portsdown Hill shows the Paulsgrove housing estate nearing completion. However, it is the background of the picture that shows the greatest amount of change. Whale Island, with its huge transmitting aerials and the long thin strip of the torpedo testing lake, dominates the view. Now the entire area of land in between has been reclaimed and the Port Solent marina has taken over, with its homes, boardwalk, cinema and restaurants.

About the Author

Anthony Triggs is the author of six previous books on the history of the Portsmouth area. By profession he is a sub-editor with the *News* at Portsmouth, and in addition to local history he is interested in family history and photography. Anthony lives at Portchester with his wife Sue.